Sugar Uncoated

A to Z

Dr. Diedra Price

ISBN: 9798995627104

"If you don't understand racism/white supremacy, everything else that you think you understand will only confuse you."

— Neely Fuller Jr.

DEDICATION

For the ancestors, whose dreams were suppressed and silenced, whose creations were taken, enriching others and giving rise to systems of power and economic wealth, whose bodies were held in captivity, exploited, and violated, their labor building wealth and empires, yet still made a way for me to speak Sugar Uncoated truth.

SANKOFA

Sankofa is a Ghanaian principle that teaches us to return and reclaim what has been forgotten or taken, so we can move forward with intention. Represented by a bird reaching back to retrieve what is behind it, Sankofa honors the past as a guiding light, grounding memory and movement as we return to voice, to speak truth from our lived experience.

A

Audacious, courageous ancestors freed themselves

over arrogance anchored and moored to shores beyond America.

B

Basking in folk telling tales of powerful rituals and rich traditions over books banned by those who will not read.

C

Challenging deceptive innocence

of Jane Crow South

over consistently emasculating the will of our people.

D

Drenched in the flawless beauty,

and antiquity of Blackness

over defunding our future and weaponizing our past.

E

Endurance and indestructibility
over elimination and erasure.

F

Fully and sufficiently human

over forty-one shots into the unarmed,

crying out for mama.

G

Gasping for more than forty acres of autonomy

over glaring colonizers besotted with occupied lands.

H

Hallelujah, touching the hem of grace

over hope falling faster than faith.

I

Inclusivity intricately braided into America's values

over infusing ignorance into institutional policies and practices.

J

Joy refreshed and reinvigorated
over "justified" impunity—
the breathtaking knee on our neck.

K

Keepers and defenders of historical truth over knowledge that is distorted.

L

Love transforms humanity

over liberated hate that lingers and drips with rage.

M

Mesmerizing bravery

over menacing actors

whose ships wrecked trafficked bodies.

N

Nestled in the warmth of diversity

over nostalgia coursing through the

cold veins of inequity.

O

Obsessed with honeyed kisses of peace and harmony—

smothered in love, tough and sweet—

over systems that betray us.

P

Power that amplifies the voices

of those on the fringes of inhumanity

over precariously perched in intoxicating privilege.

Q

Quietly planning to restore

the best of we and us

over quarreling about our body, our choice, and why Black Lives

Matter.

R

Resisting preconceived notions
over reinforcing false narratives.

S

Standing in community

over surrendering to silence—

the root of complicity.

T

Treading on the toes of manufacturers of violence

over triggered hands locked and loaded,

gunning for mass destruction of safe havens.

U

Unfettered access to our histories

over unbridled racism—

as soulless as it is heartless.

V

Victorious disruptors—methodical, tenacious—

over veiled suppression that is subtle,

and painstakingly embroidered in the fabric of law and disorder.

W

Wisdom—yes, wokeness—

over white nationalists' allegiance to a washed and whitened

ideology bathed in the brutality of ethnic cleansing.

X

Xylophones strumming the heartstrings of defiance
over xenophobes ranting and raging about the unknown.

Y

Yearning to cultivate gardens we may never cherish,

but will cede bountiful bouquets to the next generation

over yoked to a legacy of devouring our innocence and labor.

Z

Zero hoarding of power and wealth

over zealous white supremacists threatened by our achievements

and emancipated voices demanding equitable political, economic, and

social power.

ACKNOWLEDGMENTS

This work is shaped by those who encouraged and supported it, who offered a place of rest, honored my perspective, withheld judgment, and lifted me so I could speak truth.

I thank Jonvieve Morris for her careful editing and for honoring the language, rhythm, and intention of this work.

I am grateful to the artists, poets, scholars, educators, collaborators, and friends who have supported this work. It lives because of you. I also honor the work of Dr. Greg Carr, Congressman Hakeem Jeffries, and Dr. Carol Anderson, truth tellers and powerful voices for the people. Their work deepens how we understand culture, identity, history, and the power of authorship.

And many thanks to my family and ancestors, my parents and grandparents, survivors of Jim Crow, whose hope created a way forward, who endured so I would have more, and who stirred my imagination and nurtured my creativity, with deep gratitude.

ABOUT THE AUTHOR

Dr. Diedra Price is a poet, publisher, and creative director, and the founder of Words Eclectic Publishing. Her work centers authorship, lived experience, and voice as a way of knowing. She also centers Black ancestral memory and movement, liberation and resistance, and cultural identity.

Her work is grounded in an enduring reverence for the beauty and depth of Blackness.

Sugar Uncoated A to Z is her debut book, a single poem that moves through Black ancestral memory and movement, carrying truth across generations.

She is building a publishing house and developing Author Clarity Sessions, Practitioner Guides, and Sugar Uncoated Conversations, and reinvesting in self-determined, under-resourced communities through her work.

Based in Los Angeles, she continues to write, publish, and produce cultural experiences that center voice, memory, liberation, and unapologetic truth.

WORDS ECLECTIC PUBLISHING

Centering Black ancestral memory and movement, and shaping narrative on our own terms.

This work is rooted in liberation and resistance, where lived experience speaks truth, uncompromising and unyielding.

We were born free, long before captivity. Global wealth took root through the captivity, trafficking, and labor of African people.

Our presence spans the world.

This story endures, resonant across humanity.

Sugar Uncoated.

www.ingramcontent.com/pod-product-compliance
Lightning Source LLC
Chambersburg PA
CBHW051408130726
47987CB00007B/2913